GREEN WHITE GREEN

GREEN WHITE GREEN

LANRE BADMUS

authorHOUSE®

AuthorHouse™
1663 Liberty Drive
Bloomington, IN 47403
www.authorhouse.com
Phone: 1-800-839-8640

Published by AuthorHouse   10/10/2012

ISBN: 978-1-4772-3771-7 (sc)
ISBN: 978-1-4772-3772-4 (hc)
ISBN: 978-1-4772-3773-1 (e)

TO MY WIFE AND DAUGHTER
OLUFUNTO AND DARASIMI
BADMUS

Acknowledgement

I will surely spill the blood of my pen to appreciate everyone that has contributed to the Success of this project.

I will start with the Almighty Jesus Christ who is the major source of my talent and inspiration.

Then my parents; Elder Jide Badmus and Mrs Leah Badumus who sponsored me through school and gave me a solid educational background.

My sweet siblings, Jide, Bukky and Oyinlola who have Supported this dream.

Not forgetting Mr Femi Afariogun whose expert opinion and editing has brought me this far.

To Author house united kingdom; I can Spill the last drop of my pen's blood to say thank you for the exposure to time-light.

Last and not the least, My darling wife—olufunto Badmus for all your healthy encouragement and support. I love you.

Preface

My itchy fingers are in a deep romance with my poetic pen that is arrantly admired by all men living within the bosom of mother earth.

The proud product of their romantic relationship is this piece of art which seduces your senses like beauty does to the eyes.

I have willingly written this poems to create an apparent awareness about the happenings in my dark-in—complexion country—Nigeria

I solemnly spoke my mind. I aggressively echoed your thoughts and I intelligently let loose the contents of our hearts.

Green, white, green is the beautiful colour of our prestigious flag and I persistently plead that we should desist from treating it like a rag.

No matter how candidly crazy this country seems, we must still show her a long lasting love. It is our home, we have no where to go.

Though the nation is addicted to some vices-Corruption, religious riots, assassinations . . . to mention a few.

I will forever love this country till eternity is finally given a befitting burial.

Author.

Contents

PROLOGUE

Green White Green

I hereby put my pen on paper
to write my Country this letter.
A message in poetry's dialect
that has earned a universal respect.

This is the Vivid voice of a pen-
a piece of advice to all Nigerian men.
Wise words for your ears-
I'm doing this because I care.

Cast away every candid contentment.
Instead, let your pursuit be fervent.
Stop the Stare and the fold of arms.
Or else, it will give a hurting harm.

We will be stupid and crazy
To feel we have achieved the dividends of democracy.
We will be digging our gruesome graves
if for more glory we fail to crave.

The Finish-line is still Oblivious.
To everyone, this is the obvious.
Let us fight for a genuine freedom
after which we can boast of stardom.

Success sleeps silently in our hand.

Do not let her fall and rub on sand.
It is high time we waved the national flag
and stop treating it like a rag.

Another Redemption Song

Newspapers may refuse to publish
but this is beyond the borders of rubbish.
A firm freedom song
from a melodious African tongue.
Government may call this treason
but for this, I have a reasonable reason.

Let us all stand on our feet
and dance to this emancipating beat.
A perfect rhythm from a poet
That is unwilling to keep quiet,
like an articulate thunder
that can put a sky asunder.

Enough of gruesome murders
by some unknown sinister leaders.
The taking of innocent lives
that were meant to thrive.
The sucking of minority's blood
by some leaders' thirsty swords.

This is another redemption song
from an African tongue.

A new Nigeria

Today may purposefully be naughty,
Carving out situations so knotty.
She may wish to suck our tears;
leaving us with conditions we can not bear.

Today may decide to make fun of us
by closing all financial doors.
She may decorate us with diseases
that starve us of a beautiful bliss.

Today may act like an adamant goat
and insist not to move like a paddle-less boat.
She may try to delay her stay
so tomorrow may not come our way.

But no matter the hindrance,
to our tune, tomorrow will still dance.
She will willingly come to our rescue
when today's time is due.

Tomorrow is a healthy hope.
Thus, till she comes, we will cope.
She has promised us a new Nigeria-
a peaceful and a comfortable area.

New Era

Sunrise is now dark-in-complexion;
there seems to be no solution.
Mornings are now clad in black garments-
a reflection of rash and brutal torments.
Days have become charcoals-
as boldly black as a mole.
Solemn songs sail the streets-
the harmony of gruesome beats.
Cries crawl on all roads
and tears tumble in folds.

Guns spit fire at will-
to them it is not a great deal.
Fire spreads like a hungry rumour-
obviously the Government is a failed anchor.
Bombs boast of rise in death tolls-
we are confused of their actual goal.
Our security is no more guaranteed-
every day we are sown as seeds.
The situation of a new era-
Our leaders seem not to care.

A Psalm For
Independence Day

When everything looks lost
like a well-sagged bust;
Hold on to the hands of hope.
And with her, try and elope.

Profound poverty patrols the nation
with no seeming solution.
Religious riots rule everywhere,
this pathetic pain, we can no longer bear.

When everything looks lost
like a well-sagged bust;
Hold on to the hands of hope.
And with her, try to elope.

Corruption crawls around the country.
Like ants around the bark of a tree.
Assassinations arouse our sorrow.
It hurts like a poisoned arrow.

When everything looks lost
like a well-sagged bust;
Hold on to the hands of hope.
And with her, try and elope.

Kidnapping is the order of the day.
It is another vice that has come our way.
Football's beauty is also fading;
Our happiness seams to be aging.

When everything looks lost
like a well-sagged bust;
Hold onto the hands of hope.
And with her, try and elope.

Letter to Nigeria

Another blood spillage
that will remain over an age.
Another merciless murder;
you still need not bother.
I am still the arrogant assassin-
as creative as the word 'sin.'

My poetic pen gradually dies
but she is starved of sinister cries.
Her death will give you life
like bees do to their hive.
I am killing my pen for your sake
So you could eat and have your cake.

With her blood, I wish to write
this letter on this paper, really white.
A message to my nation, Nigeria;
a country with beauty really rare.
Words woven with wisdom-
it will lift you out of boredom.

Though the profound prowl of poverty
eats deeper into the national polity;
Though the platform of our leadership
intentionally imitates the titanic ship,
Light still stands behind the tunnel-
death awaits our sinister spell.

Our help, in Shackles

It seems all love is lost
as our leaders are drowned in lust.
Their care has collapsed in cascades;
this may continue for decades.

Our leaders have murdered their oaths.
Of their wealth they can only boast;
as their integrity has been assassinated
and their conscience, candidly dead.

Government laws and policies
amount to Judas Iscariot's kisses.
And we feel boldly betrayed
as dead days gradually decay.

Those we vehemently voted for
keep man-handling the law;
just to sooth their desires and wishes.
Thereby causing us irreparable itches.

Our help seems to be in shackles-
so obvious on his wrists and ankles.
Apparently we have to embrace our fate
like a fish caught by a hook with a bait.

Lamentation of a Nigerian

Everything seems to stand still
like the beautiful idanre hill.
The wind has refused to blow.
The sun has stopped to glow.

Situations seem so frozen
like thick clouds that can't be broken;
Activities have assumed a position;
they have refused to be set on motion.

A candid clog on my wheel of progress-
my zeal has gone on recess.
Circumstances seem so static.
This is really pathetic.

This ought to have become better
but I am still starved of laughter.
Situations still remain the same
and I don't know who to blame.

Something must be done in haste
or else I become a prey for fate.
Things must return in motion-
that is the sole sane solution.

Jos Mayhem

The continuous cascade of cries
like that of cloudy skies.
The tumbles of terrible tears.
from faces fagged out by fear.
The wild and worrisome wails
that do not want to fail.
The pruning of future promises;
beautiful children of all ages.
The heart —beat of gruesome guns
that appear not to be done.
The profuse bleeding of knives
that have fed on many lives.
The ground has drank to stupor.
as human blood continues to pour.
The pains of a poetic pen,
writing about the wickedness of men.
A way out seems so oblivious;
A fact obstinately obvious.
I'm as confused as a rolling die-
this is no living lie.

Hospitalized Democracy

Frustrated feelings freely
and solemnly sail around
my sorrow-soaked soul.

Thwarted thoughts tirelessly
and willingly walk around
my hurt-hit heart.

Embittered emotions have
been candidly caught within
the web of my worried mind.

And my body is blighted
like the face of an impotent cloud;
that can not weep.

Pathetic pictures of the past
persistently peep through
my moaning mind.

And a song of sorrow
could not help but
find its way into my mouth.

It seems like

the birth of a beautiful yesterday
when democracy was christened in Nigeria.

Now she has been hospitalized
as she suffers from deadly diseases;
corruption, poverty, injustice, unemployment.

A candid cure
is clearly nowhere to be found
just like the moon at noon.

December Will Not Live Forever

Beer will not always be cold.
The sun will not always be bold.
Food will not be sweet always
Especially the ones of stale days.
Roads will not always be straight—
there are bends you will hate.
The cold month of December
will never live for ever.
Smiles will not always stand by you;
a times sorrow will stare and boo.

The rule in this earthly kingdom-
you win some and lose some.
We will not always have what we want;
no matter how we skillfully hunt.
So whenever we feel the hurt of life,
we must not quench the thirst of our knife
with the abundance blood.
Of priceless human blood.
There will not always be light-
a times, darkness will steal our Sight.

Things fall apart.

Situations are no longer at ease.
Fear now resides in the heart of peace.
Calm seems so scared;
a nation with Characteristics so weird.

Things have ferociously fallen apart
as doom is desperate not to depart
this consistently cursed country of ours
for the birth and death of in-coming hours.

Chaos crawls with confidence
as dangerous as the sting of vengeance.
Everything is upside-down;
So ugly like a wicked frown.

I wonder where our help resides-
better still where she hides.
Our help seems scared of this danger
thus she stares from afar.

Our leaders continue to fumble
as the nation continues to crumble.
My tears trail in torrents
as my heart remains in rents.

Thinking about
Nigeria

Sleep seems so scared to seal
my eyes with unconsciousness.
It has taken to its heels
faraway from me like
the scorching sun does at night.

The day just dropped dead
like a rotten fruit from a tree.
It was hit by the bullet of time
and its corpse lies on the ground;
covered by the garment of darkness.

Since vigil has vowed
to hold my eyes hostage
and demand my sleep as ransom,
thoughts start to pile on my mind
like the rubbles of a tsunami.

Your thoughts have made my mind
a city of refuge for themselves.
They move around with confidence.
You are a country so rare and
I can't stop thinking about you.

Political Barbarians

Words wage war on one another
within the confines of my mind's boarders.
Lines are at logger-heads
inside my pen's blood; really red.
Poetry persistently pushes them out
as words of peace, no doubt.

A message to the Nigerian nation
looking for a political solution
through a candid and credible election
that will ease the national tension.
These words as subtle as a kiss
can never hurt a swarm of bees.

Election has come and gone
like a disappeared, dead dawn.
Let us drown our grudges and anguish
because there is no Victor and no Vanquish.
Let us blind-fold our guns and swords
and let us let loose warm words.

We should be united as Nigerians
and fight all political barbarians

In the Name of Democracy

I have persistently tried
and endeavored to hide
my frail feeling
which has rejected every healing.
But it still remains as obvious
as sunrise that cannot be dubious.

I wished I could cover my emotion
as apparent as the face of an ocean.
But the sinister stab of failure
on my wishes will entertain no cure.
Happiness watches from a distance
as sadness engages me in a romance.

Everyday I struggle to swallow it-
even if it means bit by bit.
But success stands faraway
as failure mocks me day after day.
It has become vividly unbearable
for my heart that seems` Vulnerable .

In the name of political struggle,
they keep killing people.

They fashion several weapons
and permit death to have fun.
They are determined to defend democracy
but their actions are apparently crazy.

They remain thorns in our flesh-
these wounds seem forever fresh.

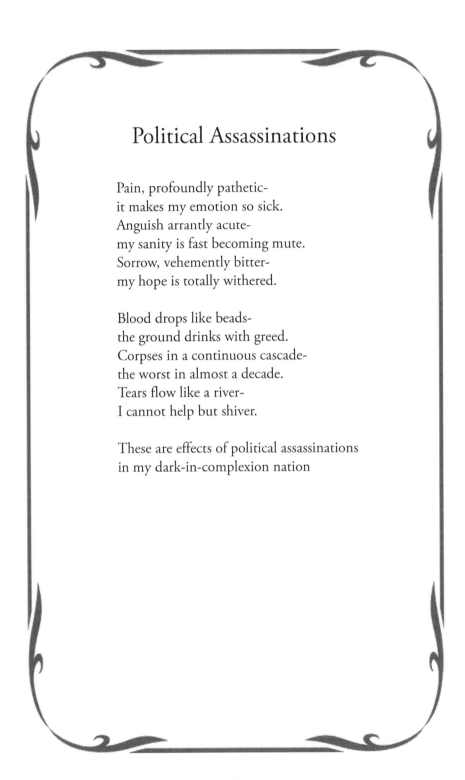

Political Assassinations

Pain, profoundly pathetic-
it makes my emotion so sick.
Anguish arrantly acute-
my sanity is fast becoming mute.
Sorrow, vehemently bitter-
my hope is totally withered.

Blood drops like beads-
the ground drinks with greed.
Corpses in a continuous cascade-
the worst in almost a decade.
Tears flow like a river-
I cannot help but shiver.

These are effects of political assassinations
in my dark-in-complexion nation

Poetry at a Cemetery

Another art of poetry.
A performance at an American cemetery.
Lines, stanzas and word's in harmony-
they cannot just be lonely.

A perfect poem from a mind
trying to put a past behind.
Lovely lyrics from a soul
with an anguish-dug hole.

Rivers of inspiration insist to flow.
Winds of ideas continue to blow.
My brain beckons for more-
it is an addict to the core.

Thus I'll persuade my pen to write
a poem with a body so bright.
It is in honour of victims of September eleven.
These souls now reside in heaven.

Though they are gone like a season.
We still have a reasonable reason
to always remember them
though they are now of another realm.

Romancing fun

Should we allow our nation to bleed
due to our gruesome greed?
Should we allow the flow of her tears
under the day's eyes so bare.
For our selfish reasons
we allow sorrow to harass her every season.
Now her pains know no bound;
as she slowly slumps to the ground.
Nigeria once blessed with profound peace
is now starved of beautiful bliss.

We claim to love her
but we willingly make her suffer.
For our selfish interests,
we make her plight to be at her best.
The abundance of our agonizing actions
is as conspicuous as the Atlantic ocean.
No one is willing to change
even as time dies of old age.
The nation nonchalantly cries on
and our leaders are romancing 'fun'

Faded Beauty of football

The constant cascade
of terrible tears
as rude and as rash as
that of a cloudy sky.

The persistent pierce of pain
through a heart already weak.
Just like a long nail
through an old garment.

The cause of my agony
and my taunting trouble
seems not for-fetched.
like stones beneath the sand.

All sectors and ministries
in my nonchalant nation
are candidly crashing
like books from a falling shelf.

Our only healthy hope is dying.
Football's beauty is
fastly fading like
the charm of a setting sun.

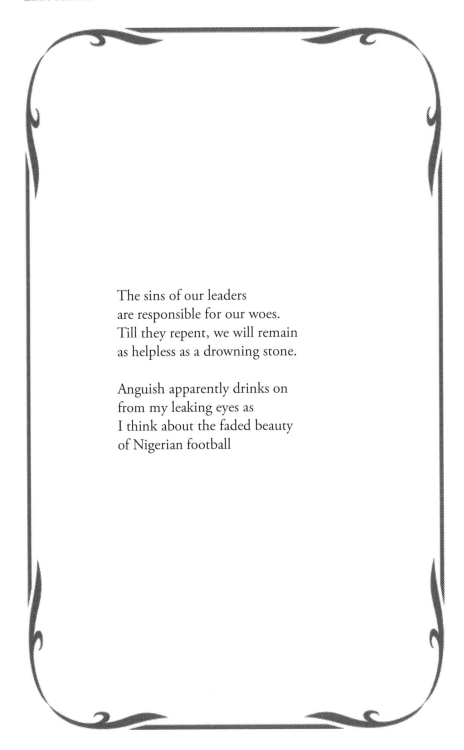

The sins of our leaders
are responsible for our woes.
Till they repent, we will remain
as helpless as a drowning stone.

Anguish apparently drinks on
from my leaking eyes as
I think about the faded beauty
of Nigerian football

Corp Members

A poem for the dead corp members-
the victims of Nigerian politics.

Life may sing a song of sorrow
to slice your joy into shreds.
Life may paint a picture of pain
to assassinate your happiness
Life may stage an act of agony
to drown you in a dam of despair.
Life may say some sinister words
to pin you on a wall of worry.
Life may write you a pathetic poem
to set ablaze your aspirations.
Heaven remains your refuge
where your pains will be totally healed.

A poem for the dead corp members-
the victims of Nigerian politics

Sunrise in South Africa

The sun silently rises
without any sign of crises.
It is sunrise in south Africa—
obviously seen, near and far.

The day boldly breaks
without any trace of aches.
It is day-break in Soweto-
candidly clear is her ego.

The streets seem so happy.
This we can all see.
Sweet and special songs
from several melodious tongues.

Our drums can't help but speak
of Africa's beauty at its peak.
Our vuvuzela can't help but proclaim
a land armed with fame.

Our culture, our wealth, our women,
apparently admired by all men.
Let me talk of her bold beauty
that is starved of everything filthy.

The world now resides in Africa
and her lands are not getting weaker.
An experience really beautiful-
a fact known even by a fool.

PHILOSOPHY

Wishes and Realities

I wish I could stop some things
I did not do in my teens.
I wish I can stay clean
like a heart without any sin.
I wish I can kill this guilt
whose soul is filled with filth.
I wish I can stand upright
as I engage these habits in a fight.
I wish I can stay profoundly pure
no matter how these vices lure.

Well, I do not think I am able
because everything now seems impossible.
It is like writing in the rain
or sailing on a ground so plain.
Building one's house on snow
or shooting a bullet with a bow.
These are just mere wishes
that end up in life's ditches.
Some things are better not started
like things that are better not said.

Make Yourself Smile

You can not fail to fall down
like a free-flowing gown.
You can not do but be on the ground
like the setting sun so round.

You are always feeling dejected
like a well-bowed head.
You keep being bitter
like a plant that can't help but wither.

Pessimism patrols your mind
and within you, it will soon unwind.
Optimism has opted out of your life
as you have decided not to strive.

All wicked words weigh you down
and all you do is frown
Foolishly, you forget about your focus-
you have taken it as your cross.

All you need is a strong heart
to withstand future darts.
Human tongue is a biter bile.
You just have to make yourself smile

Life is Just Life

Life cannot help but be life.
Cool, crazy and cowardly.
She cannot help but be herself.
Hurting, humorous and heady.

Life is a deceitful person.
She smears your face with a smile
and before the death of another hour,
She strikes your eyes with tears.

Life is just life.
As confused as amphibians,
She allows happiness hop around you
and still wishes sorrow could stay.

So why bother about life.
when she is not sure of herself.
Why cry like a potent cloud
when she cannot account for her actions.

An advice from my poetic pen
arrantly admired by men.
View life the way you wish
and that is the way it will be.

Today and Tomorrow

Today's trial try and bear
because tomorrow is obviously near.
Resist the ferocious fang of fear,
So your tomorrow, it will not tear.

Today's pains, try and endure
because she is armed with a cure.
Do not kiss the lips of failure
But hope for a successful future.

Today's ailing health
will soon lead to her death.
Tomorrow will then stand strong-
her rein will surely be long.

Today's plight
will soon lose her might.
And after the convulsion of tonight
tomorrow will come with light.

Do not give up on today
even if trouble comes your way.
Tomorrow stands at a corner-
your joy's hide-out is not that far.

Dreams are meant for Tomorrow

My dream drags on
like a crawling Chameleon.
It moves at the swift speed
of an annoying snail.

My dream wishes to fly
like the restless time.
But its wings seem broken-
flying is a ferocious farce.

Despair's desperate stare
gradually gets sterner.
But I will not give in
to its poisonous fangs of failure.

I will keep feeding my dream
with hope, optimism and luck.
And I am sure that one day,
It will turn to a hawk

Dreams are meant for tomorrow.
It need not hatch today.
Very soon it will come true
like the words of martin Luther.

Life is a woman

Life is a woman
admired by every man.
It takes a relentless fool
to think she is perfectly beautiful.
It takes a man with a slain sanity
to think always wanting her is not vanity.

Her beauty really bold
will prompt you to want to hold.
But when she comes close,
You will refuse another dose.
We can not actually do without her
and without her, you cannot go far.

She sells you a sweet smile
and after a little while,
she makes you embrace stress
under a devilish duress.
An ugly finger you cannot cut off.

Life is salient to every man.
and for everyman, there is need for a woman.

When Dreams wither

When dreams willingly wither,
life becomes boldly bitter.
When aspirations assume awkward positions,
Situations seem to be without solutions.
Hope becomes clearly helpless
like a setting sun placidly scorch-less.
You will wish death could come to your rescue
so your pains could be subdued.

When dreams desperately die,
life is a wingless bid that cannot fly.
Life becomes a boat with no paddle;
She helplessly becomes idle.
Conditions candidly turn sour
like a fermented flour.
Despair digs into ones heart
like a root down the earth.
And you wish you were a prey to death
as you stare with eyes really wet.

When Money Makes Fun of You

The persistent prowl of penury
is a bullet's bite on one's body.
The pathetic path of poverty
is as thorny as the stage of puberty.

Whenever my pocket goes lean
like the patronage of an old inn.
Whenever my purse gets dehydrated
like the body of the dead . . .

Then, the truth dawns on me
like the morning sun that must see;
When money makes fun of you,
all drastic things, you will want to do.
Poverty is nothing but a pest
that puts your patience to test.
You just want a way out—
you can do anything no doubt.

The persistent prowl of penury
is a bullet's bite on one's body.
The pathetic path of poverty
is as thorny as the stage of puberty.

I will Touch The Sky

Sternly I stared at the sky
wishing I could willingly fly.
She seems so far away
like the Biblical judgment day.
I longingly looked on
like a concentrating gun.
Endlessly hoping to have a touch.
I even dreamt of a careful clutch

Still standing, I gazed
and in me optimism grazed.
I candidly craved for a moment
when reality will ease my torment.
When destiny will allow me smile
with teeth as clean as tiles.
That day still stands at a corner
like that festive month of December.

Though the sun do set
and seasons experience death,
my own faith will never fail
and my will never derail.
The sky is still within my reach
even as I am buried in this ditch.
And till I finally touch it,
I will never rest a bit.

Profound Pain, Gorgeous Gain

Follow your humble heart
like a spear chasing a hart.
Obstinately obey your mind
because it is never blind.
Skillfully and tirelessly hunt
for what you willing want.
And don't let the dew of depression
dampen your agile determination.
No matter how weak you feel,
hold on to the hands of your zeal.
Let her lead you on,
even if you are not having fun.
Good things do not come easy—
they come along with being busy.
Listen not to what people say,
Or else you will miss your way.
Try and trudge on
and till you make it, do not be done.
With a profound pain
comes a gorgeous gain.

ROMANCE

Statement On Oath

Let the rivers refuse to run,
my love for you will still burn.
Let the sun stop to rise,
my love will still be wise.
Let roses cease to be red,
your home will still be my bed.
Let the rude rains refuse to fall,
I'll still be at the beckon of your call.
Let the mountains refuse to stand,
your love will make me understand.

If I should lose my fame
and forget about my name,
for the sake of love.
Then it is a problem I need not solve.
Many women I have met
but you are the best, I can bet.
I'll forever lavish my love on you
even if the world should boo.
These are statements on oath
which I will willingly wrote.

No Reason to Cry

Closed are all marriage doors-
for better and worse.
To this I solemnly swear.,
leaving you I dare not dare.

Try as much to believe this.,
my love's breath will never cease.
She is blessed with good health;
just like the rain forest belt.

Even if the sun goes blind at noon,
my love will still be a full moon.
If the wind refuses to blow,
forever my love will glow

Till I die with my wedding ring,
your praise, my love will still sing.
If breath still remains in eternity,
I will love you in profound perpetuity.

Tirelessly, we will thrive together.
No one will put an asunder.
In the arms of love, we will die-
thus there will be no reason to cry.

Romantic Harm

This is a lucid love letter.
No one can explain better.
A message from my soul,
in it please do not pitch holes

At the very first
I felt it was lust.
But now I can clearly see
that together we will forever be.

Oblige me a look into your face
and happiness will romance me for days.
Let me put my head on your breast-
It is a comfortable place of rest.

I wish to place a kiss on your lips
and also have them for keeps.
Please allow me an embrace
and my heart will never stop to race.

Your lovely and lively love
which fits like a hand and glove
leaves a lasting taste on my tongue.
just like the sound of a sweet song.

An apparent shadow

My humble heart heeds
the bold beckon of your beauty.
My sweet soul obeys
the clarion call of your love.
My mature mind mows
through the garden of your thoughts.
My taciturn tongue is
accustomed to your name-
a name with the body of a rainbow.
I thought I could live without you
but the truth is a sky so blue-
living without your beautiful being
amounts to a sacrilegious sin.
Staying within the bosom of life
without your persistent presence
is an accomplished suicide mission.
May I never leave your vicinity again
like the sun in romance with noon.
Your are my apparent shadow,
together we will always walk.

Twin Sonnet

I

Beauty so bare and bold-
a gift for you till you get old.
Skin so soft and spotless-
few ladies are this blessed.
Smile so sweet and tender;
a bait for the opposite gender.
Legs really long and straight;
I can no longer wait.
I liked you when I saw you-
my soul will forever woo.
Thought about you the whole night;
as I experienced romantic bites
Wish you could be my friend.
Please try and comprehend

II

Beauty on a body so bold-
can not fade even when you get old.
Skin so soft and spotless-
seems as perfect as chess.
Smile so sweet and tender;
an obvious fact even to a pretender.

Legs really long and straight-
touching them is my fate.
Loved you when I met you-
the world could willingly boo.
Dreamt about you the whole night-
sensual pictures I'll never fight.
Come and be my lone lover
And we'll be together till the death of 'forever'.

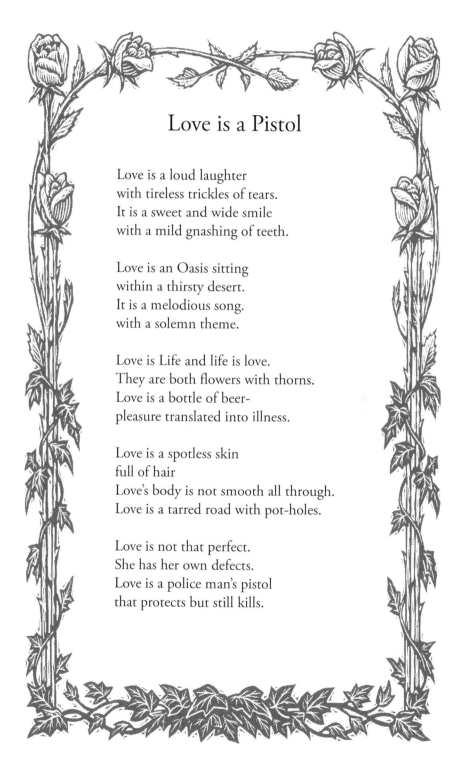

Love is a Pistol

Love is a loud laughter
with tireless trickles of tears.
It is a sweet and wide smile
with a mild gnashing of teeth.

Love is an Oasis sitting
within a thirsty desert.
It is a melodious song.
with a solemn theme.

Love is Life and life is love.
They are both flowers with thorns.
Love is a bottle of beer-
pleasure translated into illness.

Love is a spotless skin
full of hair
Love's body is not smooth all through.
Love is a tarred road with pot-holes.

Love is not that perfect.
She has her own defects.
Love is a police man's pistol
that protects but still kills.

Sent From Above

Though your heart dishes out hate.
like a beautiful but poisoned bait.
I will still willingly wait
and assume it's an act of fate.

Though time taunts and torments
me with no plans to relent.
I am still hell-bent
to remain within patience's tent

I have personally decided to endure
my pains and wait for the cure-
which is your love so pure.
Of this fact, I am apparently sure.

I am however pleading again.
Do not let my waiting be in vain.
Cut short the life-span of my pain
and treat not my request with disdain.

My weighty worry you can solve
by reciprocating my lasting love.
Around you, my life will forever revolve
because you're an angel sent from above.

A toast to our marriage

In this lovely life
blessed with a stern strife;
If you allow love to lead the way;
the sun will always rule your day.

This is a firm fact,
with an immense impact.
It is a curious truth
that digs deep like a tap root.

Like rivers Benue and Niger
that are from sources at par,
We met at a confluence of friendship
and we embarked on a journey so deep.

The road was really rough
and moving smoothly became tough.
The world inquisitively watched
and prayed we survive the scorch.

Hand in hand with love we moved
and situation impatiently improved.
Love was our capable captain
and him alone, we swore to retain.

Now we are at the alter
and no one can put an asunder
Till the death of eternity.
we shall uphold our holy matrimony

An African Angel

All hail the high heavens
for this gorgeous gift given.
An adorable angel
that made my heart revel.
Five-feet, five inches
she stands with a beauty that can't cease.

Eyes as bright as Sunrise-
they can't be accustomed to crises.
Her smiles seems so perfect
with a set of teeth without defect.
Fine and flawless figure-
I can't help but adore.
She speaks with a sensuous stammer
that makes my composure falter.
Skin so soft and smooth-
apparently from African roots.
She is the sole definition of beauty-
beauty that is not filthy.
She will be my only wedded wife
till 'forever' loses her life.

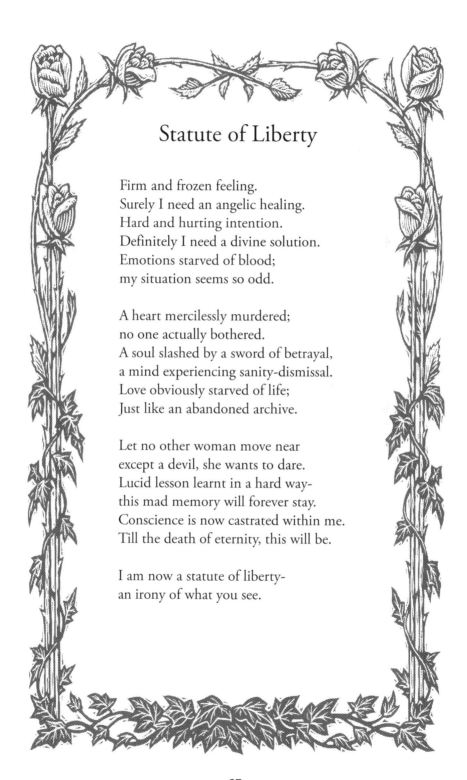

Statute of Liberty

Firm and frozen feeling.
Surely I need an angelic healing.
Hard and hurting intention.
Definitely I need a divine solution.
Emotions starved of blood;
my situation seems so odd.

A heart mercilessly murdered;
no one actually bothered.
A soul slashed by a sword of betrayal,
a mind experiencing sanity-dismissal.
Love obviously starved of life;
Just like an abandoned archive.

Let no other woman move near
except a devil, she wants to dare.
Lucid lesson learnt in a hard way-
this mad memory will forever stay.
Conscience is now castrated within me.
Till the death of eternity, this will be.

I am now a statute of liberty-
an irony of what you see.

Love lives within thorns

I wish to willingly warn
that love lives within thorns.
A fact, candidly clear
even though hard to bear.

Love is horridly hard to find-
a visible truth to the blind.
It lives within a lovely vine-
a vine well-armed with active mines.

Apparently it is my duty
to diligently depict love's beauty-
beauty in a form so naked.
Beauty that can never be dead.

Though love is boldly beautiful
like a moon with a body so full.
It is difficult to come by;
this is not a lie.

Love lives in darkness
but her loyalty can't be less.
With trials, you will find her.
Love lives at a place not that far.

Love is a Woman

Will you willingly believe me
or doubtful you will still be,
like the success of democracy
in a nation vividly crazy.

Will you embrace my wise words
that pierce profoundly like a sword.
or will you turn deaf ears
and pretend not to candidly care.

A strong and tireless truth
that is as straight forward as a tap root.
A fact that seems so agile
like the bitterness of bile.

Love is apparently a woman
that will always attract a man.
She seems so sensual and sensuous.
For her you are always desirous.

Her body so tender to touch;
her face, really beautiful to watch.
Her luscious lips give a kind of kiss
that blesses your life with bliss.

Her words are woven with care
that can conquer every fear.
And her seemingly sleek nature
depicts beauty's real colour.

Love is apparently a woman-
an arrant attraction for every man.
She is like a mature mother
who can't do but bother

Aborted Coup

Life without you
is an aborted coup.
Your apparent absence
signifies a death sentence.

Whenever I fail to see your face,
in me sorrow can be traced.
When I'm unable to hold your hand;
I become a war-torn land.

Living all alone
hurts like a broken bone.
The pains seem so profound.
Thus my tears abound.

Wish you were here with me.
and happy I'll forever be.
Wish we were inseparable
like the Bible and parables.

Please return like a summer
and make my bed warmer.
Find a way back to my heart
and make me happy on earth.

A humble Demand

A lucid letter to a friend.
A friend, a lover, I still can't comprehend.
A mature message from a heart
hit by a romantic dart.

We met in the arms of coincidence.
and our friendship grew in confidence.
Now, thinking about you is a hobby.

Now, I want to make mention
that I have no evil intention.
My thoughts are blessed with bliss-
just like a baby's genuine kiss.

As days walk on by
and as hours continue to die,
all I see is your beautiful picture
that gives me a romantic torture.

Please let me hold your hand
as I make this humble demand . . .
allow my heart live in yours
and please shut all exit doors.

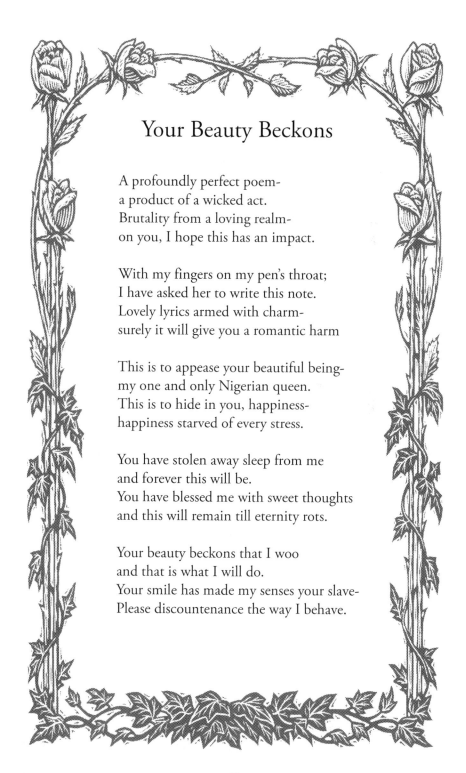

Your Beauty Beckons

A profoundly perfect poem-
a product of a wicked act.
Brutality from a loving realm-
on you, I hope this has an impact.

With my fingers on my pen's throat;
I have asked her to write this note.
Lovely lyrics armed with charm-
surely it will give you a romantic harm

This is to appease your beautiful being-
my one and only Nigerian queen.
This is to hide in you, happiness-
happiness starved of every stress.

You have stolen away sleep from me
and forever this will be.
You have blessed me with sweet thoughts
and this will remain till eternity rots.

Your beauty beckons that I woo
and that is what I will do.
Your smile has made my senses your slave-
Please discountenance the way I behave.

All I want is your hand in marriage
and we will live longer than an African adage.
Do dance to the beat of my heart
and I'll be your paradise on earth.

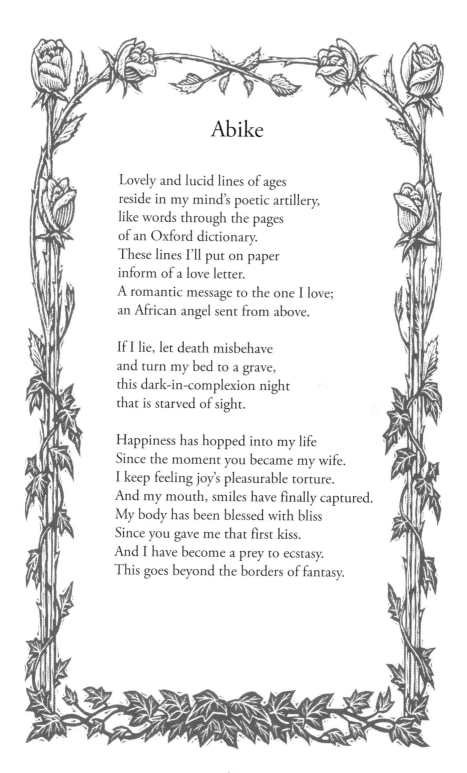

Abike

Lovely and lucid lines of ages
reside in my mind's poetic artillery,
like words through the pages
of an Oxford dictionary.
These lines I'll put on paper
inform of a love letter.
A romantic message to the one I love;
an African angel sent from above.

If I lie, let death misbehave
and turn my bed to a grave,
this dark-in-complexion night
that is starved of sight.

Happiness has hopped into my life
Since the moment you became my wife.
I keep feeling joy's pleasurable torture.
And my mouth, smiles have finally captured.
My body has been blessed with bliss
Since you gave me that first kiss.
And I have become a prey to ecstasy.
This goes beyond the borders of fantasy.

If I lie, let earth misbehave
and turn my bed to a grave
this dark-in-complexion night
that is starved of sight.

Thus I'll live and die in your arms
that is devoid of every hate and harm.
I will turn my soul to paradise
till this world finally dies.
And I will make my heart a bee-hive
where sweetness often thrives.

If I lie, let death misbehave
and turn my bed to a grave
this dark-in-complexion night
that is starved of sight.

Lost within Love
and Lust

I do not have to lie
that there is something about your smile.
Smile as wide as the Nile-
It takes my heart up the aisle.

This is a curious truth-
from your head to your foot,
you are an epitome of beauty's loot.
Apparently from an African root.

Your pretty and gorgeous face
keeps me salivating for days.
Thus, I pray for grace
to always love you till eternity decays

I can't be lost within love and lust,
till my body returns to dust.
And till forever begins to rust
loving you has become a must.

Your body speaks beauty so bare;
leaving you, I dare not dare.
You are a diamond really rare,
Thus for you, I'll always care

Love is a Rainbow

Love is a rainbow
that gorgeously glows.
Her beauty is purely bare
like an atmosphere so clear.
Her complexion is conspicuously bright
like an afternoon's sunlight.
But a fact still remains
like truth that cannot be slain-
the rainbow still has dark colours
that depict love's romantic torture.
The bright colours are the gains,
the dark taints, the pains.
Love obviously gives happiness
but she is still armed with sadness.
She is a book with a two-sided-cover;
She is seen differently by lovers.
But from any view you look at her,
your conclusion can't be that far.
Finally, she portrays her personality
in accordance with your mentality.

Plights of a poet II

If I tell you my problems,
will you solve them?
If I tell you my sick secrets,
will you keep them from the streets?
If a give you my heart,
will you pierce it with a dart?
I'm a broken tree branch
and I hope you will always catch.
I need a shoulder for my tears;
can you boldly move near.
The world has walked out on me
and lonely I have continued to be.
I am a desert's lone oasis-
my boredom will never cease.
All I have now is you-
thus I wish I could woo.
Be the smile that subdues my sorrow
and the shield against agony's arrow.
You are my only healthy hope-
to another place, please let's elope

Life without your Love

Let me let loose letters
that sooth this cold weather
Let me whisk away warm words
that romantically stab like a sword.
Let me send out stanzas that sooth
like cold waters on one's foot.
I willingly wish to write
a poem with a sensual bite.
An emotional message from a heart
hit by love's poisonous dart.
All these for a durable damsel
whose perfect beauty I can tell.

Life without your love
is a goal keeper without gloves.
This is my candid conclusion
and I need no negating suggestions.
Life without your sweet smiles
is a rough journey of million miles.
Since you silently strolled away
like the setting sun from a day,
I have become a gun without a bullet,
Obviously useless you can bet.

VARIETIES

An anthem for Poetry

Lucid and lovely lines
as expensive as Solomon's mines.
All from your lovable lyricist
who you will not reasonably resist.
A proud product of my poetic pen
arrantly admired by all men.
It is an adorable anthem
from the creative mind of a gem.
A sweet and salient song
from a melodious black tongue.
A dedication to the person of poetry
who is as creative as a cemetery.
Poetry is profoundly beautiful
like the face of a moon, really full.
So why paint of her a picture
as ugly as the eyes of a vulture.
Poetry is arrantly articulate;
her wise words apparently accurate
so why depict her as dumb
as a thumb really numb.
Poetry is a naked woman;
She is easily appreciated by every man.
So why put on her, clothes
like the fur on a gorgeous goat.
A message to people far and near-
especially to those who care to hear.
It is just a profound plea-
portray poetry as she should be.

Year 2009

On the bosom of death,
this year gasps for breath.
And I can boldly bet
that her doom will soon be met.

This year willing withers
and her end gorgeously glitters.
Lonely, her life lingers
through six-feet and yonder.

Before another hour will be born,
this frail year will be gone.
Our hearts will be filled with fun.
No one will surely mourn.

A year drunk with tears
that fell with no candid care.
In us, she instilled fear;
fear in a form so bare.

I however wish her profound pain
as she dies over and over again.
Let all her months be slain
and let her bleed like the rain.

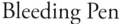

Bleeding Pen

My poetic pen bleeds
and her blood drops like beads.
She feels no pathetic pain.
She keeps smiling all over again.
My fingers penetrates her throat,
like a thirsty knife does to a goat.
She seems not to be bothered
as her blood drops on this jotter.
She will not give up her ghost-
of this I can proudly boast.

My poetic pen bleeds on
and she is still having fun.
Her blood carves out a perfect pun.
Of this, she can never be done.
Her blood is purely poetry-
as creative as an African cemetery.
She bleeds because of my readers.
About her condition, please don't bother.
Her blood gives hope, love and peace-
comfort and motivation that can not cease.

Melody of Death

I have tried to talk
as my soul seems to sulk.
My expression prays for emancipation
as my heart weeps like an ocean.
I am bleeding from within
and the flow is very keen.
My pains prick like a thorn;
all alone I solely mourn.
No one seems to understand me,
irrespective of my profound plea.
Why should they always get me wrong
like dictators do to freedom songs.
They intentionally don't comprehend
every simple signal I send.
All sensible things I say
must walk through the wrong way.
I have solemnly searched for tears
but none seems to be near.
I just want to cry out my pains
like a sky letting lose the rain . . .
my efforts have lost their breath-
they've danced to the melody of death.

High Court Judge

So many butchered years,
this one is really rare.
I have never seen such beauty
in the line of my legal duty.
Her face; gorgeously gentle
within a court of legal battles.
Her words were tender.
You will always want to hear her.
Boldly black and beautiful;
her body as luscious as wool.
Her smile seems so seductive;
It looks arrantly addictive.
Her sleek charm and aura
sapped my sanity of every power.
Her stare supersedes perfection;
it drowns me in a romantic ocean.
She is a judge of a High Court.
Imagine what she is worth.
She is obviously older than me
but with her I love to be.

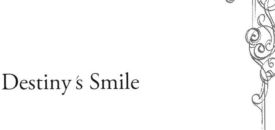

Destiny's Smile

Tired tongue.
No more freedom song.
I have taken to fate
like fish to a bait.
Looks like destiny's smile
has turned me senile.
I can not fight no more,
I'm an obvious victim of this war.
I can not find sleep.
All I do is willingly weep.
Being bullied by boredom
in this ferocious form,
is a thrust knife
that takes one's life.
Loneliness pushes me to a wall
and I have remained so dull.
I have tried to sing
but I'm a bird with a broken wing.
All freedom songs have eloped
and in pains I've been enveloped.

You are still my Eagles

You are still my super eagles
whether I'm married or single.
Your love resides in my heart
like filth in a ferocious fart.
Your picture will forever peep
into my mature mind really deep.
This love will live in perpetuity
like the life-span of eternity.

Though you were lowly rated,
your struggle is still appreciated.
The wind will not always blow west.
A times success needs to rest.
I saw your intended determination
but failure's fang had no solution.
You aimed to touch the sky,
but your wings were weak to fly.

From your sorrow, I wish to share.
This pain, let us together bear.
You once blessed me with happiness,
why won't I partake in this sadness.
Our roads can't always be straight-
that is the promise of fate.
I once benefited from your fame,
now, I can have a bite of your blame.

This world can never Smile

If this world so wild
and desperately defiled
can be allowed to dance in style;
at least for a wishful while,
then I am ready to die.

If this earth, so vile
and bitter, like a bile
can be smeared with a smile
at least for the duration of a mile,
then I am ready to die.

If this planet, prone to guile,
ruse, treachery and lies
can be pulled out of her deceitful aisle,
at least for the duration of Soyinka's exile,
then I am ready to die.

My tears flow like the Nile's
as she experiences nature's chide.
My wishes are in ugly piles-
this world can never smile
even for the journey of a mile.

Sleeping Pen

My skill slips away
like the sun leaving a day.
My passion is getting porous
and everyday it is getting worse.
My zeal loses her breath-
She falls on the bosom of death.

As each day loses her might
at the sinister sight of night;
I become as restless as money
and situations seem not to be funny.
My heart races like that of time
and with fear, I dine and wine.

Poetry has left my domain
and this has paved way for pain.
My fingers solemnly stare-
Their anguish is boldly bare.
My poetic pen still sleeps
and I cannot help but weep.

Anxiously I await the return of poetry
into my mind, as creative as a cemetery.

Seduction with no Solution

Another natural seduction
has attracted me with an addiction.
And I'm in search of no solution
to this affectionate affliction.

So sweet is her smile
that exposes her dentition so agile.
It sends my sanity on exile
and my calm, on a pilgrimage of miles.

Her fair skin is so smooth
and her body, beauty soothes.
In all sincerity and truth,
She's an embodiment of beauty's loot

I can stare for days
at her arrantly attractive face.
Her appearance sets my soul ablaze
and on me, love is allowed to graze.

I am ready to lose my lovely life
if it's what it takes to make her my wife.
This addiction really thrives
like a bee's obsession to its hive.

Another natural seduction
has attracted me with an addiction.
And I'm in search of no solution
to this affectionate affliction.

NATURE

Cold Night

The callous claws of cold
is having a strong hold
on my beautiful body as weak
as a baby's kick.

Shivers silently set in
like the swift steps of sin.
Apparently I am becoming vulnerable
like bursting bubbles.

I try to candidly cuddle
but solutions remain a puzzle.
The cold carelessly crawls on-
its like she can't be done.

My wife is faraway from home
and in me loneliness roams.
My pillow can't give the needed warmth-
thus my doom will be prompt.

My fate I have however embraced
like a shoe to her lace.
I'm already a prey to cold-
terribly strong is her hold.

Gone with no Trace

This rude rain
is at it again.
It has gone on exile
of many miles.
Gone with no trace-
can't even see her face.

The reason is as unknown
as the reason behind thunder's groan.
Her absence poses a trouble
that makes our hearts to fumble.
The repercussions are in piles
like abandoned anachronistic files.

Food hastily hops away
as hunger has come to stay.
So wild is famine's laughter-
no one can caution her.
The ground dines on, on our corpses
as we die of different diseases.

Our aggression arrantly burns
as we pray for the rain's return.

Murdered Sun

Seems like a sad story
I can no longer bury
in my humble heart-
just like waters from the earth.

The sun just dropped dead
like a corpse on a bed.
She is gone to the world beyond.
She is no more blonde.

Apparently we are all aware,
but no one seems to care.
We obviously did not bother
about how she got murdered.

From all reasonable reasons,
the sun was a good person;
because she gave us sight
unlike the dark-skinned night

Now our doom is bound
as she remained buried in the ground.
Darkness will soon reign
and we will have nothing to gain.

Seems like a sad story
I can no longer bury
In my humble heart-
just like waters from the earth

Nightfall

The dark sky drags on.
She is definitely not done.
Her heart is heaped with fun
like a sentence spiced with pun.
The moon is still timid-
to her hide-out she still heeds.
The stars are still on exile
and the sky remains undefiled.
Serenity seems so brave.
For her composure, I'll forever crave.
She remains speechless
to avoid any manner of mess.
This night is virtually beautiful-
an apparent fact even to a fool.
She silently stares;
devoid of all fears.
She depicts an African woman
Who is the toast of every man.
This revelation is however my duty-
Nightfall is armed with arrant beauty.

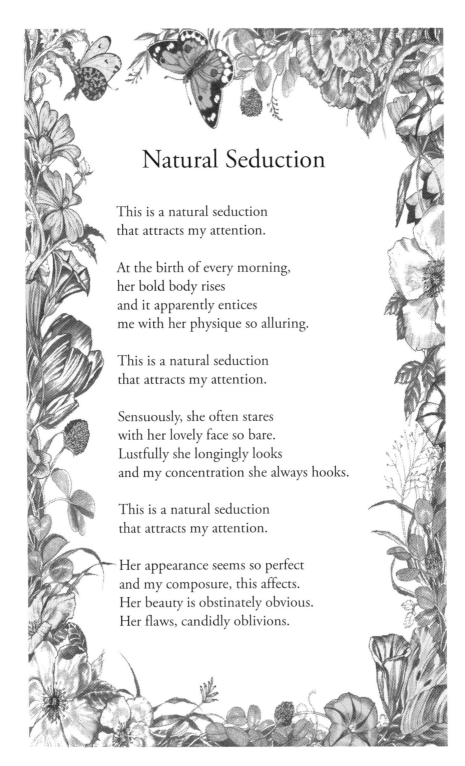

Natural Seduction

This is a natural seduction
that attracts my attention.

At the birth of every morning,
her bold body rises
and it apparently entices
me with her physique so alluring.

This is a natural seduction
that attracts my attention.

Sensuously, she often stares
with her lovely face so bare.
Lustfully she longingly looks
and my concentration she always hooks.

This is a natural seduction
that attracts my attention.

Her appearance seems so perfect
and my composure, this affects.
Her beauty is obstinately obvious.
Her flaws, candidly oblivions.

This is a natural seduction
that attracts my attention.

But soon, she will set-
of this fact, I can bet.
Her seduction will stroll away
like a bullet gone astray.

A natural seduction
that once attracted my attention.

When calm came calling

A severe storm once struck
before the crow of the cock.
The sun was still asleep
when the sky started to weep.
Her tears tumbled in torrents
and we were scared for our tents.
The wind wildly wandered
and our hearts, fear conquered.
The rain lashed on with her might;
and chaos stood at sight.
My bed, with a body really nude
was no candid place for refuge,
but I held onto it
like a baby holds a tit.
Hours piled on hours
and down came the sinister shower.
But when calm later came calling
like sunlight in the morning;
I had every cause to glorify God
who delivered me from every odd.

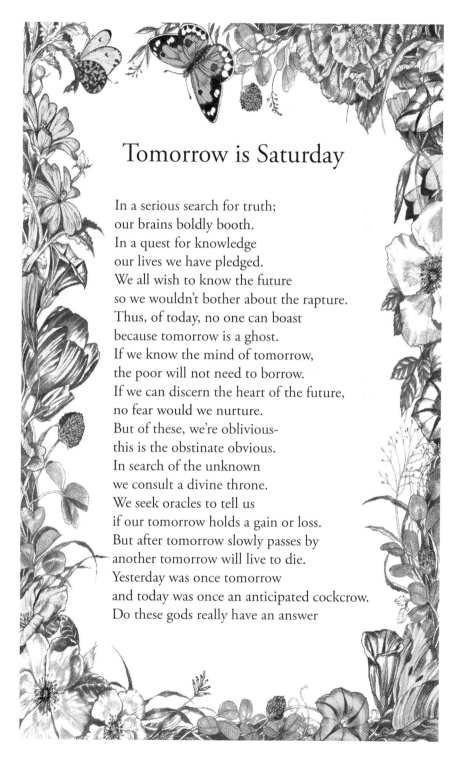

Tomorrow is Saturday

In a serious search for truth;
our brains boldly booth.
In a quest for knowledge
our lives we have pledged.
We all wish to know the future
so we wouldn't bother about the rapture.
Thus, of today, no one can boast
because tomorrow is a ghost.
If we know the mind of tomorrow,
the poor will not need to borrow.
If we can discern the heart of the future,
no fear would we nurture.
But of these, we're oblivious-
this is the obstinate obvious.
In search of the unknown
we consult a divine throne.
We seek oracles to tell us
if our tomorrow holds a gain or loss.
But after tomorrow slowly passes by
another tomorrow will live to die.
Yesterday was once tomorrow
and today was once an anticipated cockcrow.
Do these gods really have an answer

before the death of another December?
Tomorrow is still a mystery.
no matter the words of philosophy and history.
Tomorrow is Saturday-
another tomorrow may be Monday.

Lagos Flood

For years, these waters were mute
like a drowned, helpless flute.
Now they are apparently angry
and for revenge, they seem hungry.

For decades, we infringed on their rights-
be it by day or at night.
We treated them like slaves-
restricting their tides and waves.

Their legs, we consciously crippled
and they became weak and feeble.
We be-headed their freedom-
they were as speechless as a torn drum.

Now the waters are mad-
they are hell-bent to make us sad.
They have retaliated with floods;
working wonders like Moses' rod.

For years, these waters were mute
like a drowned, helpless flute.
Now they are apparently angry
and for revenge, they seem hungry.

The fall of a Night

The day in now as blind
as an obviously bias mind.
And darkness diligently drags on;
night surely seems to be having fun.

Serenity strolls around with poise-
no one could hear a single noise.
Peace parades with pride
and chaos has gone to hide.

The fall of the night is a blessing
to every present persons.
We could feel the touch of calm-
its as soft as a baby's palm.

The death of the day
has brought rest our way.
Now we can silently search for sleep,
and have her for keeps.

The return of the night
has murdered our plights.
Now we can heave a sigh of relief
and experience some reprieve.

Another Irony
of Life

Another irony of life-
Her terrible and torrential tears
make us as happy as the sun.
Her solemn and sound sighs;
as loud as a gun's heartbeat
assures us of an agile joy.
Her candidly cruel cries
smear our faces with strong smiles.
And it exposes our teeth
as white as the body of the moon.

The sky's sorrow-stricken soul
attracts us with great ecstasy-
because her arrant agony is apparently
a big blessing in disguise.
The cloud cries on in pain
and our laughter is definitely not in vain.
Our farmlands feed on these tears,
so why should we bother.
Let sadness patrols her heart in perpetuity-
it is just another irony of life.

Sonnet for Sunrise

My fingers make a candid cuddle
under a crying candle.
My pen is the victim of the romance
and their love, darkness has enhanced.
They seem as silent as a cemetery
but they both dissect the world of poetry.

It's a sweet sonnet for sunrise;
I think three stanzas will suffice.
She appears with a face so bright
like stars on the body of the night.
Her beauty seems so obvious-
her boldness, candidly conspicuous.
Sunrise is clearly perfect-
it deserves a poetic respect.

Beaten by the Rain

I was beaten silly
by a brutal bully
at the fall of yester night
that was starved of light.
Her whip whisked around
my body that seems round.
And her cane
caused me profound pain.
Several strokes stung me
and angered I continued to be.

The rude rain lashed on.
She really caught her fun.
I cuddled myself in shame
as I had myself to blame.
I knew the cloud would cry
from the thunder's continuous sighs.
But I still boarded a bike
and went on a romantic hike.
Now I have been beaten silly
by a brutal bully.

A new Day

Dusk drastically drowns
in the warm waters of nature,
like a war-battered town
gets buried in agony's torture.
Dawn raises her head
as the sun strolls out of bed.
Light lingers around
and a lovely day is bound.

A day blessed with the sun's smile
as wide as the mouth of Nile.
An atmosphere armed with bliss
as harmless as a genuine kiss.
It possesses profound promises
of happiness that cannot cease.
A new dawn that harbors hope-
hope that will never elope.

Apparently, it's another lovely day
that has willingly walked our way.
We have no other choice
than to revel and rejoice.

Cloud Cries Again

The Cloud cries again
like a troublesome toddler
being whipped with a cane
by her strict mother.

Her tears tirelessly tumbles
as her emotions continue to fumble.
She weeps at will–
her pains, she cannot conceal.

Her sorrow seems to be our joy
like babies delight in toys.
For her tears we prayed
as hours continued to decay

It has been long we saw her cry
just like a leap year gone by.
Thus, we wish she can cry forever
Probably till next year's November.

May her trouble never be halted
and her anguish never be dead.
May the cloud cry in perpetuity
I mean till the fall of eternity.

A cloud without Tears

An apparently truth
as obvious as a ripe fruit
has stared me in the face
for the past dying days.

A ferocious fact
which made my body to react,
still stands strong-
it cannot be wrong.

Since you were gone
like a bullet from a gun;
I've been a night without the sun-
my life has been starved of fun . . .

I've been the sun without her scorch.
Weakly, I continued to watch.
I have become at body with no breath-
Obviously in love with death.

I've been a fish with no gills-
hope you know how that feels.
I have been a cloud without tears
and you seem not to care.

Now I know that without you,
my deadly doom is due.
Thus I'll pray for your return
like a year about to be born.

Sonnet for the Rain

The night seemed so bright;
courtesy of the moonlight.
The moon stood, with poise;
She stared without any noise.
Darkness seemed so scared
but the moon never cared.
She painted the sky white
with her garment of light.
Though she looked lonely
amidst a sky not homely-
She beamed on with boldness
and intimidated the shy darkness.
The full moon is indeed beautiful;
an obvious fact, even known to a fool.

Once upon a Night

No matter how the day threatens,
this night is forever strengthened.
Darkness drags on with confidence.
as light has lost her coherence.

This night has come to stay
as the day has misplaced her ray.
A night much expected-
my anxiety seems so naked.

This night suffers from the claws of cold;
thus my lust has grown really bold.
Passion piles on one another
and my heart-beat has become louder.

My composure is candidly altered
as my calm cannot help but falter.
Lust lingers in my soul
and it burns like a red coal.

These memories will live till eternity
and these cravings will go beyond my city.
A night of raw romance
when lust was enormously enhanced.

Last Sunday's Rainfall

Night continued to decay
and a sober Sunday came our way.
From her heart starved of bliss,
tears tumbled with ease.
From her soul, sobs sounded
like snores from a bed.
Her plights, we could not figure out
but her pains was not in doubt.
My roof also wept along-
it all sounded like a solemn song.
The wind's breath was as calm
as a man begging for alms.
And trees gently cried.
as if someone just died.
These tears ran helter-skelter
through gaudy gutters.
And the ground got drunk
from excess of tears so conk.
Through it wasn't a rude rainfall,
our Church service seemed so dull.

A simple Answer

Your heart habours a question
like a pregnant cloud keeps the rain.
Your soul secretes a curious thought
like a broken wall hides a lizard.
Why me, in a classroom blessed
With several gorgeous girls?

My answer is as apparent as
the scorching sun at noon.
And as Obvious as harmattan
in the month of December-
you are as beautiful as
a sky stained with a rainbow!

The Rain is Drunk

An apparent fact
which will make you react
stands strongly on its feet
like the melody of Marley's beat.

The rain is Obviously drunk
from nature's breath so conk.
It seems to be starved of sanity
like a war-stricken city.

The rain rudely runs.
It seems to be catching fun.
In fear we stare
but the rain never cared.

It lashed on with malice
and clearly, it won't cease.
It has lost its composure
and chaos is sure.

The rain is placidly drunk-
a fact you can't debunk.
Let us take to our heels
before it decides to kill.

EPILOGUE

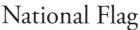

National Flag

Smile surrounds my mouth;
this is pure joy no doubt.
Brightness beholds my face;
it has stayed put, for days.

Happiness harasses my heart
like a hunter with a killed hart.
Joy jumps around my soul
like footballers celebrating a goal.

The reason is the sun in the sky
obstinately obvious for every eye.
Am I still meant to talk?
Alright, please let us have a walk.

I have finally spoken my mind
as I've left nothing behind.
A poetic word is enough for the wise;
especially the one starved of lies.

This naughty nation it still ours;
though situations have gone sour.
Let's still be proud of our national flag
and stop tarnishing it like a rag.

About the Author

Lanre Badmus is a legal practitioner and he owns a law firm in Nigeria. The young man who is 30 years of age is not strange to the writing world. He is poet, novelist, playwright, columnist . . .

His first published book is 'GORGEOUS MURDER' which is a collection of poems. He was a regular columnist for the Sun Newspaper Nigeria between 2005 and 2008. His column was entitled 'The Lyrist' and there, he displayed his poems.

Lanre Badmus who is also a radio presenter and popularly called boy friend on radio is also a columnist with SYMBOLS MAGAZINE. He is married to Funto Badmus and he has a daughter called Darasimi Badmus. His hobbies-broadcasting, writing, playstation . . .